First Facts®

SCIENCE **BASICS**

WHAT IS SOUND?

by Jody S. Rake

Consultant:
Paul Ohmann
Associate Professor
College of Arts and Sciences: Physics
University of St. Thomas

PEBBLE
a capstone imprint

First Facts are published by Pebble,
1710 Roe Crest Drive, North Mankato, Minnesota 56003
www.mycapstone.com

Library of Congress Cataloging-in-Publication Data
Library of Congress Cataloging-in-Publication data is available on the Library of Congress website.
ISBN 978-1-9771-0269-0 (library binding)
ISBN 978-1-9771-0508-0 (paperback)
ISBN 978-1-9771-0274-4 (eBook PDF)

Editorial Credits
Jaclyn Jaycox and Mari Bolte, editors; Kyle Grentz, designer; Eric Gohl, media researcher; Laura Manthe, production specialist

Photo Credits
Capstone Studio: Karon Dubke, 20–21; Shutterstock: Anton Havelaar, 9 (bottom right), Daxiao Productions, 15, deedeenaja, 7, EarnestTse, 5, f11photo, cover, ilusmedical, 13, India Picture, 9 (bottom left), inspiron.dell.vector, 19 (cell phone & tower), Jemastock, 19 (satellite), Litvalifa, 9 (top), Mike Monahan, 19, Roman Voloshyn, 17 (back), saicle, background (throughout), Sermchai PurnPorn, 8, Trofimov Denis, 17 (inset)

Printed in China.
966

TABLE OF CONTENTS

SOUNDS
ALL AROUND

Birds chirping, cars honking, friends laughing. Every minute of the day you hear sounds.

Sound happens when an object moves or ***vibrates***. The vibration pushes on groups of atoms called air ***molecules***. These molecules bump into other molecules. This action is called a sound ***wave***. The sound wave travels through the air to your ears.

vibrate—to move back and forth quickly
molecule—the atoms making up the smallest unit of a substance
wave—energy usually moving through air or water

FACT

Sound waves travel 1,125 feet (343 meters) per second. That is almost the length of four football fields!

SOUND IS A WAVE

Sound waves travel in all directions. If you throw a rock into a still pond, it makes ripples. The ripples move out in growing circles. The circles then start to fade. Sound waves work like this in air. The further you are from the sound, the weaker the waves are.

LOUD AND SOFT, HIGH AND LOW

Different sounds are caused by different sound waves. Louder sounds create larger sound waves. Quieter sounds create smaller sound waves.

Sound waves determine a sound's ***pitch***. Higher-pitched sounds have a higher ***frequency***. This means they vibrate many times each second. Lower sounds vibrate more slowly.

pitch—how high or low a sound is

frequency—the number of sound waves that pass a location in a certain amount of time

FACT

There are some sound waves that only animals can hear. Dogs have much better hearing than we do. They can hear high-pitched sounds that we can't.

Loud

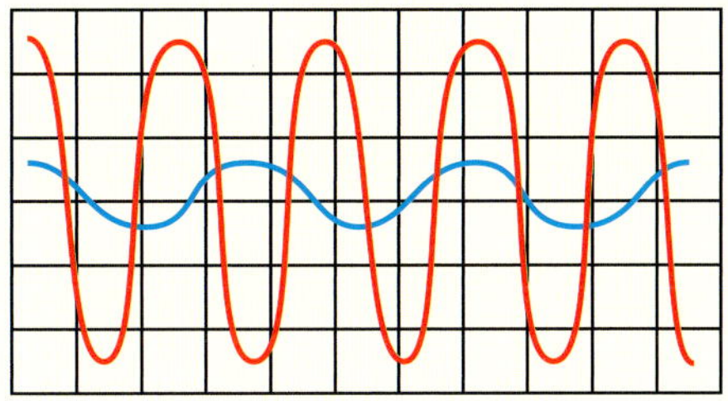

Soft

Low Frequency

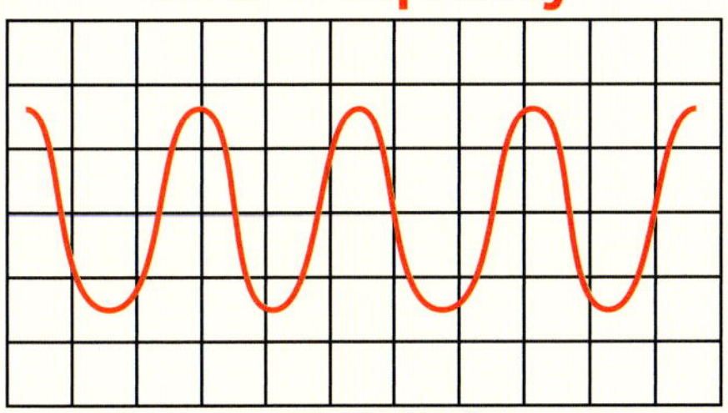

Low Pitch

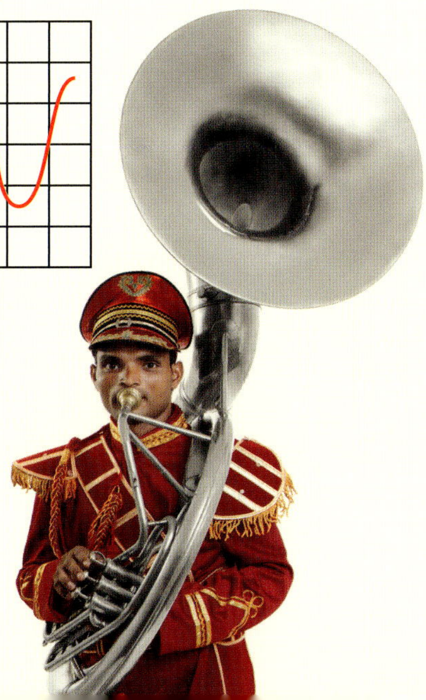

High Frequency

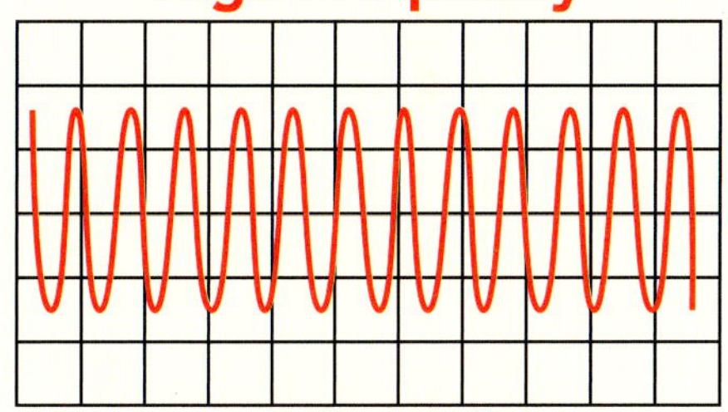

High Pitch

SOUND THROUGH **AIR, LIQUID, AND SOLID**

Sounds can travel through more than just air. They can go through liquids and solids too. Molecules in liquid are closer together than they are in air. This allows sound waves to travel faster and farther in liquid. Molecules in solids are even closer together than in liquids.

OCEAN ECHOES

Dolphins use sound to communicate with each other. They also use sound to help them learn. This special type of sound is called echolocation. A dolphin sends high-pitched whistles out into the water. The sound waves bounce off objects. They echo back to the dolphin. This lets the dolphin "see" objects. The echo tells them how far away and how big the objects are.

FACT

You would not be able to hear sounds in outer space. There is no air in space. So there are no molecules for the sound waves to travel through.

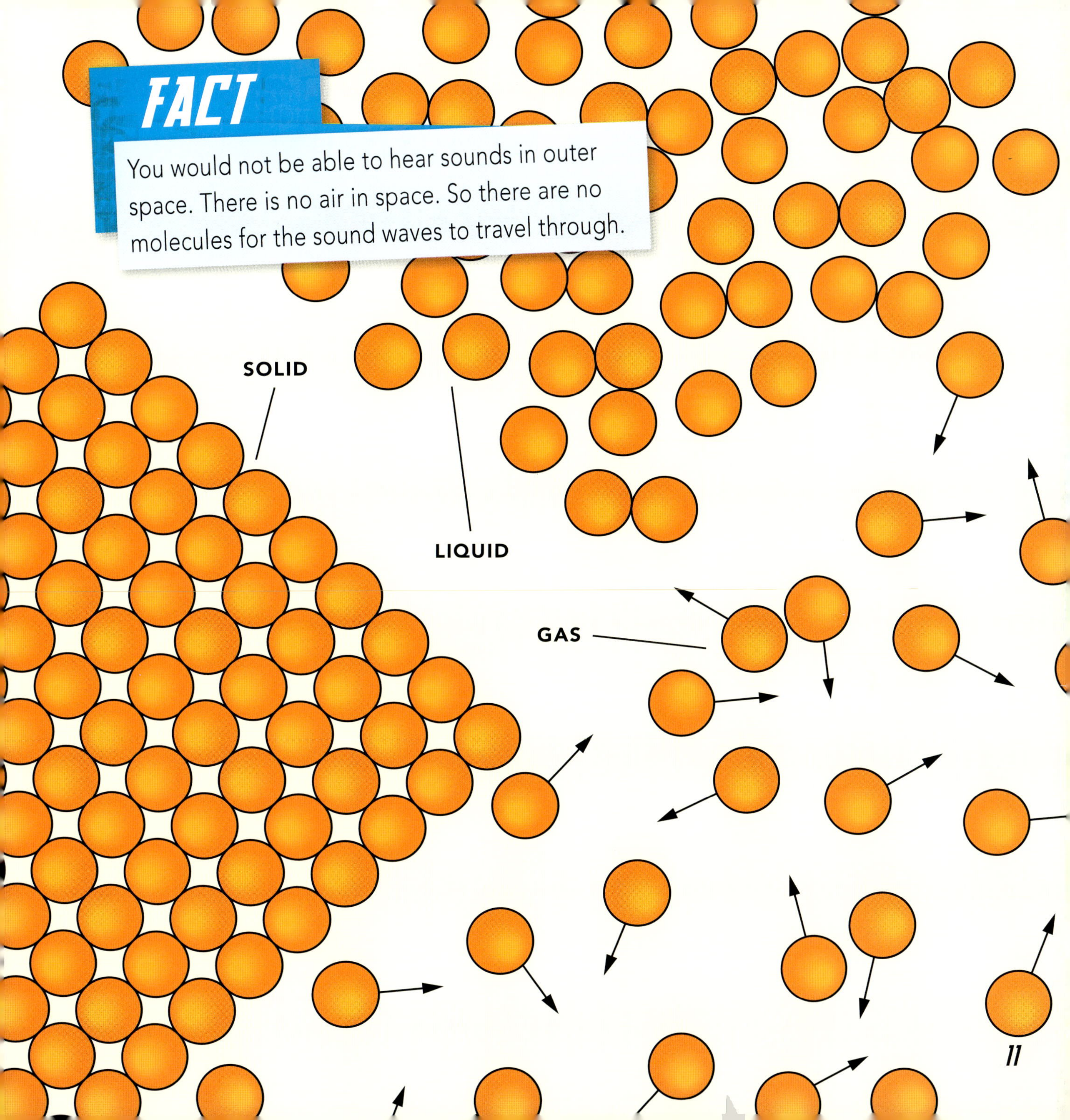

RECEIVING SOUND: **HOW EARS WORK**

Our ears are designed to receive sounds. Sound waves reach the eardrum and tiny bones, causing them to vibrate. The bones carry the vibrations to the ***cochlea***. The cochlea is in the inner ear. It contains thousands of very tiny hairs. Different sounds make different hairs vibrate. ***Nerves*** attached to the cochlea pick up the sound. The nerves then carry the sound message to the brain.

cochlea—a spiral-shaped part of the ear that helps send sound messages to the brain

nerve—a thin fiber that carries messages between the brain and other parts of the body

DIAGRAM OF AN EAR

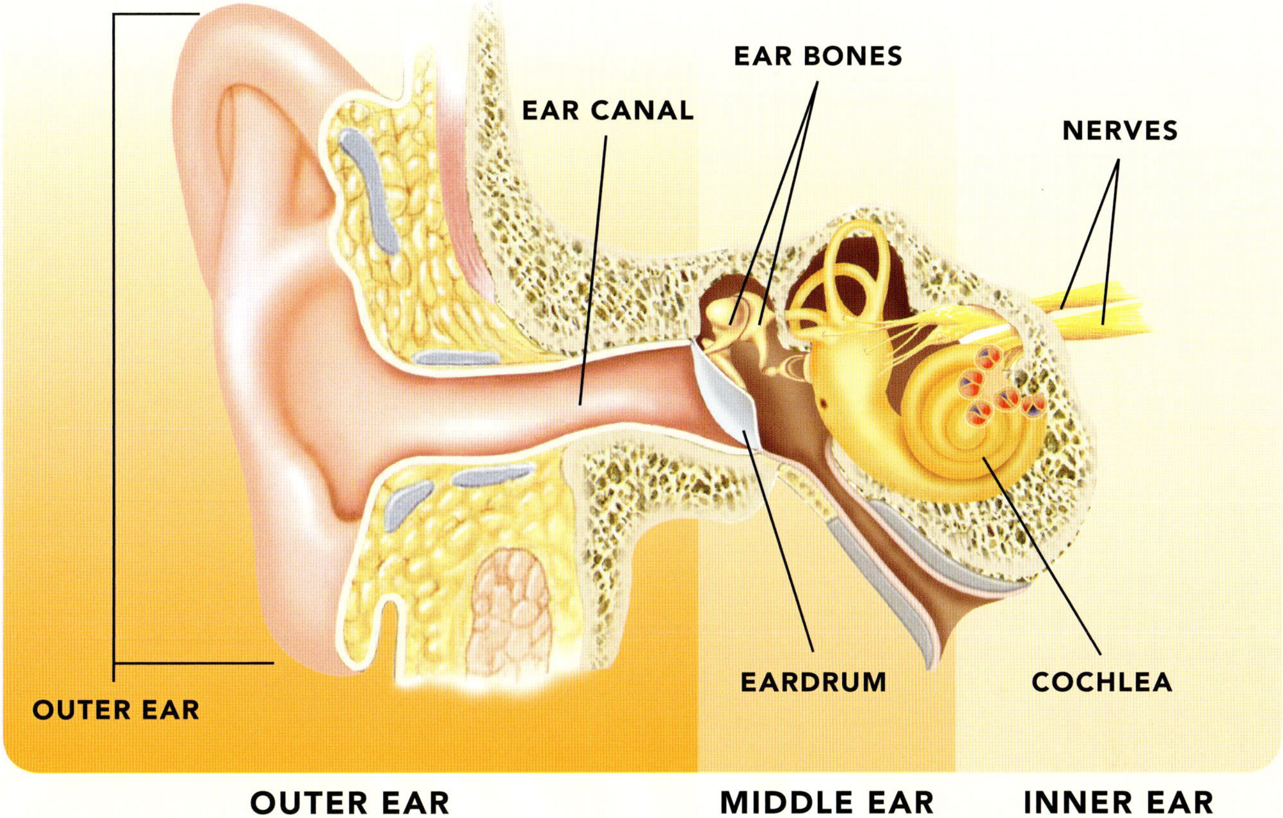

FACT

People who have trouble hearing often use hearing aids. These small objects fit inside the ear. They use a tiny microphone called an **amplifier** to make sounds louder.

amplifier—a piece of equipment that makes sound louder

SOUNDS FOR **COMMUNICATION**

Sound is an important part of communication. Animals and people make sounds to communicate with each other. A baby's cry tells its mother that it is hungry. Sounds can also give us information and warn us of danger. A school bell tells us it's time for recess. A fire alarm warns us to get to safety.

SOUNDS AND MUSIC

Musical instruments make sounds in different ways. Stringed instruments work by plucking or rubbing the strings. Different lengths of strings make different pitches. Woodwinds and brass instruments work by blowing air through a tube. You hear high or low sounds by controlling the opening in the tube. ***Percussion*** instruments make sound when you strike them. You hear different sounds based on the instrument's size, shape, and material.

percussion—instruments that create sound when they are struck or shook

FACT

Acoustic guitars have hollow wooden bodies. The air space inside the guitar make its music louder. Electric guitars usually do not have hollow bodies. They use electric amplifiers to make sound louder.

acoustic—music not enhanced by an amplifier

HOW PHONES WORK

When you speak into a phone, a microphone turns your voice into an electrical signal. The signal from a wired telephone travels through wires. A cell phone signal travels through the air. The signal is then turned back into sound by the other person's phone.

TURNING SOUND INTO TEXT

Computers can turn the sound of your voice into text on a screen. A microphone receives vibrations made by your voice. It turns the vibrations into small sounds a computer can understand. The computer compares these sounds to a huge library of words in its memory. Then it turns the information to text.

FACT

Cell phone signals travel to cell towers. Some cell towers send the signals to a **satellite** in space. The satellite bounces the signals back to other cell towers. This whole trip takes less than one second!

satellite—a spacecraft used to send signals and information from one place to another

SOUND EXPERIMENT

OBSERVE SOUND WAVES

MATERIALS:

- plastic wrap
- medium glass bowl
- 1 teaspoon (5 milliliters) cornstarch
- 1 teaspoon water
- small glass bowl
- spoon

WHAT YOU DO:

1. Stretch plastic wrap across the top of the medium bowl and seal it tightly. Make sure there are no wrinkles.
2. Mix the cornstarch and water in the small bowl with a spoon until smooth.
3. Scoop a small amount of the cornstarch mixture over the plastic. It should be close to the middle. If there are any bubbles, lightly touch them with your fingertip to pop them.
4. Get your face very close to the bowl. Hum loudly. Do you see anything happen to the cornstarch?
5. Gently touch your fingertips to the plastic covering and hum again. Do you feel anything?

SOUND TRAVELING THROUGH A SOLID

MATERIALS:

- metal dinner fork
- wooden table
- watch or timer
- a friend

WHAT YOU DO:

1. Holding the fork loosely by the end of the handle, strike the tines (pointed end) on the table. What do you hear? How long does the sound last? Repeat this step and time the sound with your timer.
2. Put your head down on one end of the table with your ear touching the surface. Have your friend strike the fork on the other end. Then immediately touch the tip of the handle to the tabletop. What do you hear? How long does it last? Repeat this step using your timer.
3. You can also experiment with different types of surfaces (metal, plastic, glass, or stone). Which surface does sound travel through the best?

GLOSSARY

acoustic (uh-KOOS-tik)—sound not enhanced by an amplifier

amplifier (AM-pluh-fy-uhr)—a machine that makes sounds louder

cochlea (KOH-klee-uh)—a part of the ear that helps send sound messages to the brain

echo (EK-oh)—the sound that returns after a traveling sound hits an object

echolocation (eh-koh-loh-KAY-shuhn)—the process of using sounds and echoes to locate objects; whales and dolphins use echolocation to find food

frequency (FREE-kwuhn-see)—the number of sound waves that pass a location in a certain amount of time

molecules (MOL-uh-kyool)—the atoms making up the smallest unit of a substance; H_2O is a molecule of water.

nerve (NURV)—a thin fiber that carries messages between the brain and other parts of the body

percussion (pur-KUH-shuhn)—instruments that create sound when they are struck or shook

pitch (PICH)—how high or low a sound is

satellite (SAT-uh-lite)—a spacecraft used to send signals and information from one place to another

vibrate (VYE-brate)—to move back and forth quickly

wave (WAVE)—energy usually moving through air or water

READ MORE

Braun, Eric. *Curious Pearl Masters Sound: 4D, an Augmented Reading Science Experience*. North Mankato, Minn.: Capstone Press, 2019.

James, Emily. *The Simple Science of Sound*. Simply Science. North Mankato, Minn.: Capstone Press, 2018.

Marsico, Katie. *Sound Waves*. My World of Science. Ann Arbor, Mich.: Cherry Lake Publishing, 2018.

INTERNET SITES

Use FactHound find Internet sites related to this book.

1. Visit *www.facthound.com*
2. Just type in 9781977102690

CRITICAL THINKING QUESTIONS

1. The frequency of sound waves determines how high or low a sound is. What is this called? Hint: Use your glossary for help!
2. Do sounds travel faster in air or in solids? Explain your answer.
3. Explain the process of how hearing works.

INDEX